The Love Book

The Hazelden Meditation Series

Twenty-Four Hours a Day

The Promise of a New Day: A Book of
    Daily Meditations

Each Day a New Beginning: Daily Meditations
    for Women

Today's Gift: Daily Meditations for Families

Night Light: A Book of Nighttime Meditations

Touchstones: A Book of Daily Meditations
    for Men

Days of Healing, Days of Joy: Daily
    Meditations for Adult Children

Day by Day: Meditations for Young Adults

Food for Thought: Daily Meditations for
    Dieters and Overeaters

The Love Book

Written by Karen Casey
With Illustrations by David Spohn

HARPER/HAZELDEN

ISBN: 0-86683-505-9

Printed in the United States of America

88 89 90 VPI 10 9 8 7

Harper & Row

About the book:

This collection of weekly meditations explores the topic of love between friends, family, lovers, and strangers, as well as self-love, and the challenges and new vistas love offers in any of its forms.

About the author:

Karen Casey is the author and coauthor, respectively, of Hazelden's best-selling meditation books, *Each Day a New Beginning*, and *The Promise of a New Day*.

About the illustrator:

David Spohn is the illustrator of Karen Casey's two previous meditation books, as well as many others. He lives on a farm outside Forest Lake, Minnesota, with his wife and two sons.

INTRODUCTION

There is probably no expression in my life that's been more difficult to feel, develop, offer, accept, or maintain than love. And I have so desperately wanted to revel in it, certain that if only I "knew" love, I'd be forever happy, content, and serene every moment, never tragedy's victim. How foolish our beliefs, sometimes.

My search for love didn't begin when I was a young woman. Rather, it paralleled my search for security that is rooted in my childhood. As a young child I longingly looked into the faces of others for signs of their love and thus my security. I was haunted by the fear I'd be abandoned. I was certain I was unlovable. After all, wasn't I always being criticized? What I didn't know as a child, and still fail to remember with all too much frequency is that I am loved in the purest sense of the word, and my very existence is my proof. I am a part of the spiritual universe — we are all parts of the spiritual universe which is our Mother — the whole of Love.

But we humans, in our frailty and our ignorance, fail to recognize the bigger picture of love. Instead we pin our desire for love and security on others who, like us, are crippled by their blurred vision of love's presence.

In my personal search for love, I grasped men and possessions, achievements and "causes," finally alcohol and other drugs before I came to know where love had resided all the time. I wish I could say I've never forgotten. But frequent reminders and daily moments for reflection are necessary for me to know I'm secure and loved and that all is well in my world today. Every day. Even when I'm feeling pain.

I wrote these meditations on love because I believe all of us share the same struggles with self-knowledge, thus discovering love's home, and finding the courage to be honest and vulnerable with our fellow travelers, whose lives mirror our own and from whom we desire love. I've often been helped over a stumbling block or down an unfamiliar pathway by a few thoughtful lines or a friend's well-chosen words. I hope what you read here will serve you in your search as others' words have served me in mine. Of course, the irony is that the harder we look for love, the more blurred our vision. Only when we become quiet and trust that love is our birthright do we discover its friendship has enfolded us.

In real love you want the other person's good. In romantic love, you want the other person.
— Margaret Anderson

The expression of real love is so easy between grandparents and children — and between good friends it passes effortlessly. But why is it so hard to share real love with a spouse or lover? Why, instead, do we want to possess them? And from them we dream of selfless devotion. Yet neither possession nor devotion guarantees the security we long for.

Real love is not selfish; it frees both the giver and the receiver. Knowing we're loved sustains our hearts and diminishes our difficulties. It doesn't bind us, yet paradoxically it bonds our hearts. This encouragement to grow, to change, to dare to depart if it's for our own good, are expressions of real love. Real love is never ownership, only stewardship of this moment's experiences.

Let's be gentle with one another, and love fully with trust, as a child loves a grandmother.

Unconditional love corresponds to one of the deepest longings, not only of the child, but of every human being.

— Erich Fromm

Feeling the need to be perfect to ensure we'll be loved is as familiar as the robin's whistle heralding spring. Am I too fat to be loved? Do people think I'm dumb when I speak out? Mistakenly, we feel unique in our struggles with our fears of inadequacy, thus we fail to find comfort among friends and strangers who share our selected fears.

If we could understand our sameness with others, we'd be able to feel the gentle urging within to acknowledge their presence, their smiles, their messages which are assuredly meant for our ears only. Their desire, like our own, is for the promise of love.

Unconditional love wants expression; pass it around and watch it return tenfold.

There is nothing else that can expand the human soul, actualize the human potential for growth, or bring a person into the full possession of life more than a love which is unconditional.

— John Powell, S.J.

A garden tended by loving hands reaps succulent fruits. Our attention to family and friends, when offered lovingly, likewise reaps rewards for all of us. Our efforts are not soon forgotten by us or our loved ones. Each loving act we express finds its home, in another's heart as well as our own.

The decision to love someone unconditionally is simply made — and yet it takes daily persistent effort. How quickly we forget the promised benefits. Each day a gentle reminder is needed.

"I will love wholly and nurture the fuller development of someone special." This one commitment, carried out, guarantees two vital, growing souls.

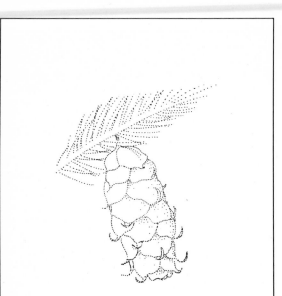

When a child loves you for a long, long time, not just to play with, but really loves you, then you become real.

— Margery Wilson

Intimacy with another is a necessary risk if we're to know love. This means loving enough to let someone in on our most hidden parts, daring to share the awful truths about ourselves. When we hold a dreaded memory within, or fail to disclose our darkest secret, we're haunted by the fear that another's love is both conditional and long gone if the truth about us is revealed.

Though seldom remembered, one of the greatest tributes we can give one another is full expression of who we were, who we are, and who we hope to become. During any single moment, we are a composite of feelings, memories, and projections. Our reality is many-faceted, and being intimate requires that we enrich each other's lives with the full expression of ourselves.

Being real is courageous; it takes a decision and practice, and it is demanded if we're to know love.

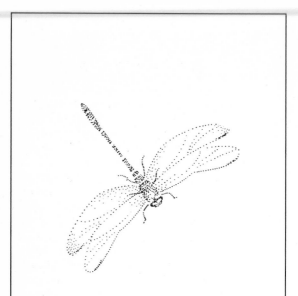

It is better to be hated for what you are than loved for what you are not.

— Andre Gide

Undeserved love haunts and shames us. And we know when we've enticed another dishonestly, or insincerely influenced an outcome. Yet we struggle letting others know more than our surface reveals.

Will I be loved if I'm really known? Our fear drives us to hide our inner, awful, human core. But then we doubt all love, all lovers, because they don't perceive the real me, the shameful me.

The dilemma is letting ourselves be known and risking that others might go away, or sharing just those parts that will endear others to us for the moment, postponing the inevitable fear of abandonment.

Serenity is the complement to a life lived with integrity — a life in which we reveal who we are each moment, trusting that unconditional love will deservedly bless us in return.

The evolution of human growth is an evolution from an absolute need to be loved towards a full readiness to give love.

— Dr. Karl Stern

As children we looked to our parents for love, for clothes and food, for an indication of who we were. If our needs were met, we felt secure. As developing adults, we still seek love. We continue yearning for security and all too often our self-definition comes through someone else. But a healthy sign of our growth is revealed each time we extend love to another with no thought that love is owed us in return.

We can show our love in myriad ways — a genuine smile, a note of appreciation, an unexpected favor, perhaps flowers, or a phone call. Warmly giving another attention in any form is an act of love, one that will be repaid in full by someone, at some time.

The ease with which we genuinely love others is directly proportional to our commitment to loving as a priority in our lives. To love is a decision first, an action second, a value next.

When we are feeling unloved and depressed and empty inside, finding someone to give us love is not really the solution.
— Gerald G. Jampolsky, M.D.

Each of us wants to be significant to someone else. And we are — we're significant to all the lives we're touching at this very moment.

The emptiness we sometimes feel is a good reminder that the women and men in our lives need *our* attention. Too much self-focus fosters our feelings of loneliness, and then with desperation we look to others to fill us up. The paradox is that we heal ourselves while offering our attention to another who is, by design, on our path.

It is not by chance our lives are intertwined. Loving someone today will heal two wounds, ours and theirs.

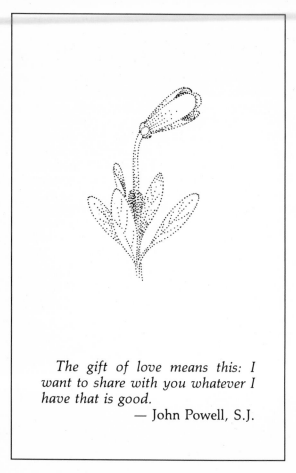

The gift of love means this: I want to share with you whatever I have that is good.

— John Powell, S.J.

How loving are we, really? Do we keep score when we do favors for a friend, keeping in mind that we're owed one? Do we hoard rather than share a favorite treat, hoping to prolong our own feast? And the good mood, when it's ours — do we use it to help another raise her spirits or do we secretly gloat because we're "in a better place"?

The opportunity to respond with love visits us throughout each day. A smile, a kind gesture, including someone in a conversation, noticing a job well done, are acts of love, acts that connect our hearts, at least for a moment. When someone has shared love with us in some form, we notice it and are moved.

Love is selfless, yet it exhilarates the self.

— Sue Atchley Ebaugh

With a quickened step we hurry toward a challenge when empowered by love. Conversely, even the simplest of experiences have the power to fill us with dread when love is absent.

Expressed to a friend, a lover, even a stranger, love promises us unanticipated gifts. We're openly appreciated, the glow of warmth enfolds us, and we find even our courage is magically bolstered when we've shared ourselves in a loving way with someone.

With ease we may express love to children, touched by their vulnerability, certain we'll not be bruised by rejection. If only we'd continue our free expression of love to all the child-adults on our paths, we'd discover both exhilaration and the courage to face any event life passes our way.

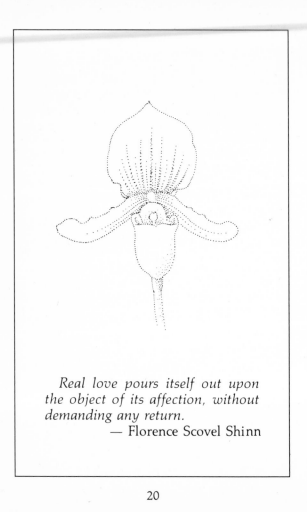

Real love pours itself out upon the object of its affection, without demanding any return.
— Florence Scovel Shinn

L oving another wholly, purely, with no strings attached promises ecstacy, and yet seldom do we dare chance it. Often we want the promise of love in return if we're to offer it. Our fragile egos are held tentatively intact by the slim gestures and fleeting words of love tossed our way. But when we bargain for love, we don't find it.

Real love will forever elude us unless we put our own selves aside and unabashedly love the self of someone else.

Freely spreading the warm glow of love to others magically invites its return — another of life's mysteries.

*To love is to place our happiness
in the happiness of another.*
— Leibnitz

To desire personal happiness is normal and healthy. Most of our plans, choices, and dreams about the present and future regarding jobs, relationships, and hoped-for achievements are geared to make us happy. It's never wrong to want happiness; however, to receive it at someone else's expense or to selfishly steal it from another will result in sorrow. And our greatest happiness will visit us when we least expect it — when we are attentively seeing to another's happiness.

Doing for others — perhaps shopping for a friend who's ill or aged, maybe offering child care to an overworked parent, or cooking a surprise meal for a lonely neighbor — will never fail to heighten our own pleasure.

*The basis of happiness is the love
of something outside self.*
— William George Jordan

S elf-centeredness destroys the very self it pur-ports to nurture. When our vision of an experience stops at the tips of our noses, we fail to notice the colorful passing panorama that promises the enlightenment for which we've been created. It's only through our interested involvement with others that we'll discover what we need to know. Perpetual introspection deprives us of the worldly information that nourishes each searching soul.

We lead muddled, directionless lives when we fail to listen to the clues for finding happiness being uttered by those we choose to ignore.

Just as we must water and thin our raspberries if they're to multiply, so must we cultivate the seeds of friendship if we're to know happiness. And attuning ourselves to the sounds of another's heart offers us a clearer perspective on our own.

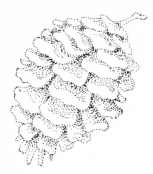

The degree to which I can create relationships which facilitate the growth of others as separate persons is a measure of the growth I have achieved in myself.

— Carl R. Rogers

A s children we clung to and modeled ourselves after friends and siblings and sometimes parents. We imitated with ease how a friend walked and gestured. At times we identified too closely, and lost the self that ached to be known. And just as often, we encouraged someone else to follow our lead. The struggle to be whole and separate and happy was consuming. It consumes us even now.

We often neglect individual development, opting instead for a closeness with others that defies real love and stifles our growth. Unless we explore our individuality, we'll neither discover nor be able to nurture the talents that are our gifts. And the truest demonstration of our love is to nurture that exploration in another.

The paradox is that finally we can only sustain meaning in our moments and hours of togetherness if we've tapped the source of our creative strength in our times apart.

We must cherish both the coming together and the going apart to know love.

Love, the magician, knows this little trick whereby two people walk in different directions yet always remain side by side.
— Hugh Prather

Destiny has its own course in each of our lives. And our movements with others who are special will thankfully be parallel at times. However, our paths will sharply intersect now and then and we'll even find ourselves at painful cross-purposes on occasion. But if the love we're expressing is part of God's plan for us and not just to satisfy the selfish ego, we'll not stray from one another's dream, though we may depart for brief periods of new growth.

We must fulfill our personal desires, vocationally and recreationally, if we are to successfully offer up our special talents for the goodness of humankind. And most assuredly that's why we're here — in this place — at this time — with these particular people.

Others cannot pull us from our true calling. If the love between us is real, it will free us and bless our direction — trusting our hearts will not be torn asunder.

The butterfly silently returns when the winds blow free.

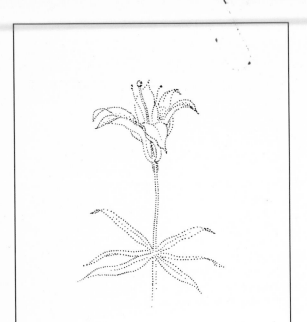

*I like not only to be loved, but
also to be told that I am loved . . .
the realm of silence is large enough
beyond the grave.*

— George Eliot

We've all heard many times that we must love ourselves if we're ever to love another. Too often we mistakenly think that means we shouldn't need to hear someone's affirmation of love. That assumption is wrong. Praise from others builds our self-confidence, keeps us on track, aware of how we're presenting ourselves moment by moment.

But many of us didn't develop healthy egos in our youth because we didn't get feedback that affirmed us. We didn't hear we were loved. As adults, we're scrambling to feel confident, to feel sure of our direction and our value to society. And we're hoping to hear we're loved. We can be certain someone close will be helped by hearing our words of love.

There's no time like the present for sharing love.

Sincere love is not born of posses-
siveness but of necessary space and
distance.

— Melanie Gainsley

Dimestore romance novels and the passion frequently portrayed in movies invite us to mimic behavior that's seldom in our best interests. Focusing attention too narrowly on another person stifles our personal growth, without which we die, as does the relationship, in time.

Real love means we will celebrate one another's avenue to fulfillment, feeling joy when our paths are parallel, trusting the growth process when our directions seem at cross-purposes. We'll know that, whatever our destination, we'll each be in the right place at the right time truly free to love one another — not forced because we've been trapped in a binding relationship mistakenly defined as love.

But where are our role models for healthy love? Few of us have been privy to them. And yet, we can discover responsible, loving behavior for ourselves if we'll risk honesty about our personal goals, our fears, our dreams, and allow our loved ones the same honest openness.

. . . love is a great beautifier.
— Louisa May Alcott

How do we feel when someone says, "I love you"? Do we feel a rush of warmth throughout our bodies? Do we walk a little taller? Do smiles come more easily to our lips? Words of love are inspirational. They bring out the best in us; perhaps they even encourage us to move in new directions, set new goals, attempt the unfamiliar.

Loving and being loved soften the hard edges of life. No stormy day is really bleak when we share it with a loving friend. No formidable challenge is too overwhelming when a loved one is nudging us forward, certain of our capacity to succeed. And the mirror reflects brighter eyes and fewer lines when we carry the knowledge that we're loved.

Let's share this knowledge with someone else now, and spread the beauty around us.

*Two persons love in one another
the future good which they aid one
another to unfold.*
　　　　　— Margaret Fuller

We can see the potential for growth in friends we love, a reality that often lies hidden to them. Through our encouragement and our commitment to them, we can help them tackle the barriers to success. Likewise we'll be helped. It's within the plan, ours and theirs, that we're traveling this road together.

For moments in time, we're matched pairs, drawing from each other the talents the world awaits, while alone we sometimes withdraw, thus depriving the world of what we have to offer. The expression of love will push forward the development of the whole human race.

No one of us is without someone to love if we'd but choose to offer ourselves to another.

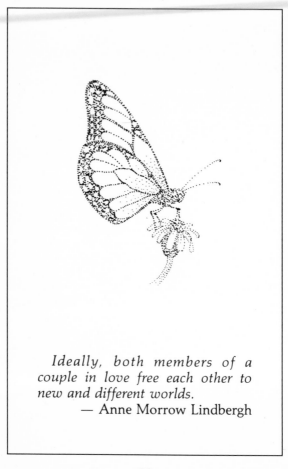

Ideally, both members of a couple in love free each other to new and different worlds.
— Anne Morrow Lindbergh

We cannot possess another's spirit, even though we may desire to do so while struggling to feel love. We must not block one another's invitations for adventure even though we fear being left behind. We won't find the happiness we long for if we've tied another to ourselves by strings of shame, guilt, or pity.

Being free to love, or not, is the only path to real love. A trapped butterfly soon loses its splendor, and life; likewise, a trapped lover quietly awaits the relationship's death.

Traveling separate, yet parallel, paths keeps a relationship vital. Bringing fresh ideas, favored hopes, and fruitful experiences to each other's attention is the enhancement a relationship must have to stay strong.

Let's not corner our partners but instead trust that real love is the promised gift of being free.

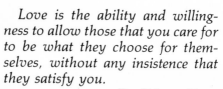

Love is the ability and willingness to allow those that you care for to be what they choose for themselves, without any insistence that they satisfy you.

— Dr. Wayne Dyer

It's generally a struggle to let a child develop a new skill, particularly if it's not one we share or appreciate. It's even more difficult to watch a spouse or lover travel a new path of learning or recreation when we're not invited to share the trip. Yet assuredly, our love is only as deep and real as it is honestly supportive of others spreading their wings to discover their own directions and personal joy.

What is right for us will never be lost or taken, and that which departs, be it friend or lover, is only making way for our own next plane of growth. We must not fear letting our loved ones experience new and separate challenges. Instead, let's rejoice in the knowledge that we each have a particular calling, a unique destiny that has brought us together and will keep us together for just as long as "the big plan" calls for.

We can't keep someone's love for us when we've made them prisoners in our homes and hearts.

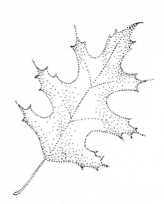

A love relationship is based on a desire to grow and to expand oneself through living, and a desire for one's partner to do the same.
— Stanton Peele

A ll too often we mistake possessiveness for love. We say, "But if you loved me, you'd go with me — you'd not disappoint me. You'd be here when I want you here." Entrapment of someone is not love. Being tightly clutched to another's bosom is not love. The paradox is that real love lets us leave; it encourages the freedom to fly on to new challenges, and to return if the desire urges us back.

We will not lose what is right for us, be it a job, a friendship, or that special relationship, so long as we honor it and acknowledge our gratitude for it. But our fears that we'll lose our significant others often drives them away because we tighten our hold and hamper their growth, thus hindering our own. Soon we have two stifled and sad people haunted by the question, "What went wrong?"

Both of us must be free to grow, to change, even to leave if we're ever to know love. Let's celebrate our separateness and cherish our moments of closeness.

Love one another, but make not a bond of love.

— Kahlil Gibran

L ove doesn't demand; love compromises. It doesn't possess; it frees. Love doesn't gloat; it praises. Love makes friends of strangers. It softens our rough edges and strengthens our assets. Knowing we're loved inspires us and invites forth our best effort. Offering our love humbles us and cultivates an inner joy.

Never, in the name of love, should we direct another person's life, but instead let's celebrate the choices made by someone dear, even when they run counter to our own desires. We are each blessed with a destiny, unique and necessary to the others in our lives. We must be allowed to travel our paths to fulfillment. Let's free one another and know real love.

Love involves a willingness to suffer and to be inconvenienced.
— Lewis F. Presnall

Love sometimes shouts and hurts, even while it blesses. The act of loving another broadens our understanding of the human condition and often pinches our egos. Indeed, one of the greatest gifts, though not necessarily cherished, which is granted through loving another is that we gain humility and thus healthier, smaller egos.

How often do we say the words, "I love you," and yet resent being detained by our loved ones? How frequently do we expect to get our own way when resolving a conflict? Is the silent treatment a manipulative ploy we commonly rely on when problem-solving with a spouse or lover?

Love wears many faces and it means not always getting our own way, or never doubting the other's sincerity. We aren't guaranteed happiness forever after, even when we know we're loved. But what giving and receiving love does promise us is growth, periods of peacefulness, some poignantly painful times, and many chances to demonstrate that another's well-being is our priority, which in turn assures us of our own well-being.

It is only with the heart that one can see rightly . . . .
— Antoine de Saint Exupery

If we look at the world through suspicious or angry eyes, we'll find a world that mirrors our expectations — a world where tension will mount, arguments will abound, strife will be present where none need be. However, our experiences in some manner bless us, and we'll recognize that if we'll look upon them with gratitude. Everything in our path is meant for our good and we'll see the good when our hearts act as the eyes for our minds.

When we see with our hearts, our responses to the turmoil around us, the fighting children, the traffic snarls, the angry lovers, will be soft acceptance. When our hearts guide the action we can accept those things we cannot change, and change those we can. And the heart, as the seat of all wisdom, will always know the difference.

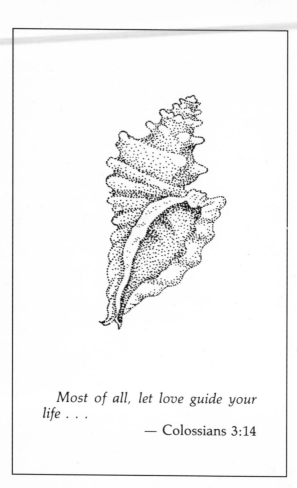

Most of all, let love guide your life . . .

— Colossians 3:14

Envy of another's good fortune puts distance be-tween us. We forget fortune visits us all, though it's frequently disguised in experiences we dread. Resentments over forgotten appointments or misplaced mementos also result in distances that discourage the growth we deserve.

How different the days will unfold when we greet each person, every experience with a warm heart, the gesture of friendship, and a calm spirit.

With feelings of love guiding our thoughts and grooming our actions, we're certain of finding pleasure in all the tiny crevices of life.

A weed is but an unloved flower.
— Ella Wheeler Wilcox

Through actively loving one another we nurture the richness of everyone's fuller expression. With no more than a nod of attention we can elicit a smile or perhaps a commitment to attempt again a challenge that defeated us earlier. None of us shines as brightly, moves as swiftly, or succeeds as easily as when someone special is rooting in our corner.

We each need someone special, and let's not forget that we are someone special to another who is walking our path. The loneliness of a day is diminished when we feel the love of someone near or far. The dread of any task is lessened when we bask in the knowledge that we are special to someone. Like roses, we bloom while under the gaze of loving eyes. Let's remember to nurture the rose within the friends and strangers who are walking our way today.

The salvation of man is through love and in love.

— Viktor Frankl

The panhandler on the busy street corner feels forsaken. The elderly woman whose phone doesn't ring stares through a gap in her drawn drapes and wonders if she's been forgotten. And awaiting the prayed-for visit from a potential foster parent, the child is fearfully certain he won't be acceptable.

The tragedy is that so few of us have experienced whole and unconditional love from the significant people in our lives. So few of us are certain of our value in the lives of others. For parents and teachers we performed to earn their favor. From friends we expected acceptance, yet sometimes we bought it. And because we haven't known the pleasure of unconditional love but have been perpetually in search of it, we've not felt adequate to offer it to others. It's difficult to give away what we fear we don't have; yet, paradoxically, that's the key to our salvation.

As we give others our love, we'll likewise experience a greater measure of it. And it need not come from outside. It will, instead, well up from within. We each have the power of personal salvation. All we must do is love.

*One of the attributes of love . . .
is to bring harmony and order out
of chaos.*

— Molly Haskell

Have we forgotten how to love in our hurried passage through life? Perhaps we need reminding that love focuses our attention and guides our direction. Our actions aren't hurried and our feelings aren't confused and unraveled when we're loving others and ourselves. Love offers form and enhancement to each moment.

When we experience the love of another, we remember our importance, and theirs, to the circle of life, and we feel encouraged, at times even impelled, to share the enchantment of love with someone new.

When the day's frantic activities crowd the heart's silent places, we must slow our pace and take notice of the loved ones in our presence, there by intent, remembering with them the design that has captured us and given meaning to our lives.

Love creates music from the disharmony of our haphazard life choices. Giving it away is like a song of happiness emerging from our hearts.

Love is the lamp that lights the universe: without that light . . . the earth is a barren promontory and man the quintessence of dust.
— Mary Elizabeth Braddon

All of us are lighted by love. Child care, car repair, concluding a report — are easier tasks when we know we're loved. We don't feel quite as alone and conspicuous in a crowd of strangers when we recall that someone special loves us. No new adventure, first plane trip, or first day of a class or new job feels quite as threatening when we've got the company of a loved one in our hearts and minds.

You might be thinking, "But I don't have a special loved one now." How narrowly we define being loved. We have friends who love us, who think of us even when we're not present — just as we think of them. And no one of us is ever away from the protective realm of a Higher Power who loves us always and everywhere we go.

Wherever we look there is someone who, like us, will find the day easier if he remembers he's loved.

Love is the magician, the enchanter, that changes worthless things to joy, and makes right royal kings and queens of common clay.
— Robert G. Ingersoll

Love invites us to perform our very best. Knowing we're loved removes the edge of terror when we're contemplating the unfamiliar, the party with strangers, or meeting a new boss.

We are transformed by love. It comforts the questioning mind and the quavering heart. We can endure the long moments of suspense while awaiting a hoped-for outcome when we know we're loved. And those times we doubt another's love, times that are sure to come, will quickly slip by if we're reaching out with a loving heart to someone else.

Every event promises greater joy when experienced with a spirit laced with love. The robin's song, the laughter of children, the vibrant colors that ooze from the petals of flowers capture our attention when we're feeling loved.

Love heals us and bonds us and promises us a life filled with moments of magic.

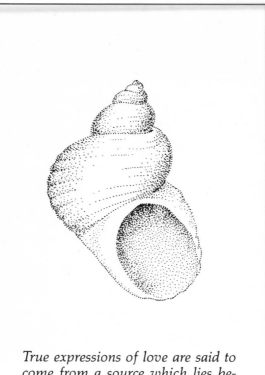

True expressions of love are said to come from a source which lies beneath words and thoughts.
                    — W. Timothy Gallwey

Remember when we just *knew* Grandmother loved us, even if she didn't say anything? Her smile or hug said it all. We can always feel another's love — when it's real.

Likewise, the words of love, when they come from a heart that's cold, don't ring true to our ears. We hear them, but our hearts can't feel them. So the gulf between us widens and we remain two lonely people.

Feeling true love for another may be foreign to us, and we may have to practice thinking loving thoughts and saying loving words to become familiar with the feelings love engenders. But real love lies deep within our center and only awaits our knowledge of it.

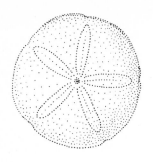

I wonder why love is so often equated with joy when it is everything else as well: devastation, balm, obsession, granting and receiving excessive value, and losing it again.

— Florida Scott-Maxwell

In our quiet moments we dream of the gifts that accompany being loved and imagine ourselves as always filled with laughter, a glowing warmth, a serene perspective. But how short-sighted our vision. Love promises us growth as well, and growth may mean a loved one's choice to depart for a time, or a struggle for agreement about future directions. Tears and fears are commonplace when we enter the realm of love.

Let's not forget that all experiences, even the dreaded ones, are meant for our good. We are never given more than we can handle, and we will be given a balanced set of circumstances. A measure of joy will follow a period of sadness. As experience has shown, quick on the heels of the fear of loss is the realization that in the spiritual realm we're secure and all is well.

How grateful we might become that love offers us so much to grow on.

*When love beckons to you, fol-
low him, though his ways are hard
and steep.*

— Kahlil Gibran

There will be many opportunities to express love in the days ahead, and some may be cloaked in harsh wrappings. Perhaps an argument will wound and then be healed by the exchange of loving words and intimate gestures.

Maybe a friend or lover will be called away for a while, and the painful loneliness will make us question our commitment to love. Yet, in loving unconditionally, we'll find peace.

Love, though a soft word and a gentle image, doesn't always promise us soft, gentle moments. Sometimes love offers us a pained heart and empty arms. We know love comforts, but not always. Love heals, but in its own time. The desire to know love draws us together, always.

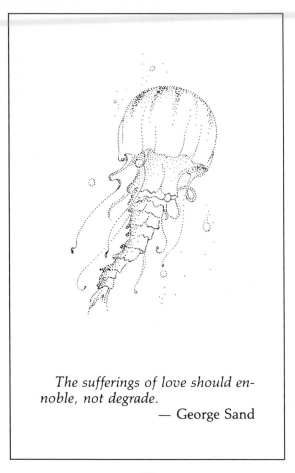

The sufferings of love should en-noble, not degrade.
— George Sand

Only in the imagination does love promise happiness forever. Through experience we discover the myriad dimensions of love. Sometimes love is joy. Sometimes passion. Sometimes moments of serenity amongst the laughter and sadness. Generally love is soft. But it also may sting. Love is forever changing, perhaps a smile will slow our pace one minute, but a sign of danger may push us to act, to respond, to make a decision the next.

All that love is, there's much it is not. Love is not shaming. Nor is it punishing. Love does not gloat, criticize, degrade, or diminish. At times we think we're filled with love and yet we selfishly serve our needs before another's. And when we truly express our love to another, there's no mistaking the warm glow that fills the body.

How simple to be a giver of love and yet how forgetful we are when the opportunities arise.

Love is an expression and assertion of self-esteem.

— Ayn Rand

How easily we love others when we feel self-assured, when we're comfortable in our chosen work, with our families and friends, with our directions in life. But the way isn't always smooth, nor should it be, and for this we can thank God, our protector and mentor.

The challenges of a rough passage confront us when it's time to grow. Seldom do we cherish the growing, and yet the gifts promised by these challenges — the increased self-awareness, the heightened sensitivity to others, the greater humility — make every moment that lies ahead profoundly more personal.

Hindsight is convincing. The paradox is that the more we trip, but pick ourselves up and move ahead with determination, the more self-assured and thus loving we'll become.

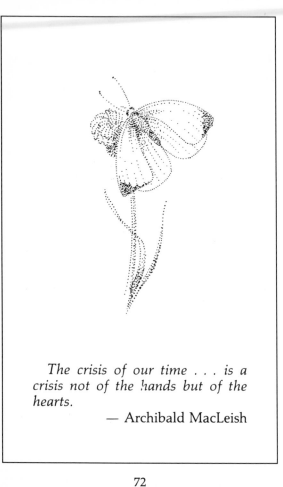

The crisis of our time . . . is a crisis not of the hands but of the hearts.

— Archibald MacLeish

We singlemindedly search for love, for belonging, for affirmation from others that will wipe out the torment of alienation that haunts our wakefulness and our dreams. "Does he truly care?" we wonder. "Did she try to call as she said?" Our fears, coupled with our loneliness, turn us inward and the seduction of isolation tightens its hold.

Our hearts plead, sometimes silently, other times hysterically, for comfort. And paradoxically, another's crisis can end our own. If we can hear the call from another's heart today, our own hearts will discover the comfort we crave.

If we look closely and with love toward the people so carefully placed in our midst, we'll discover many hearts, like our own, searching for acceptance.

Let's relieve our haunting alienation and extend a hand in love to a lonely friend today.

Love itself is not an act of will, but sometimes I need the force of my volition to break with my habitual responses and pass along the love already here.

— Hugh Prather

The familiarity of isolation is both haunting and inviting. In our separateness we contemplate the joys of shared hours with others while seeking the freedom from the pain that likewise hovers on the heels of intimate relationships. The question eternally whispering around our souls is, "Do I dare let you in, to share my space, to know my heart's longing, to feel my fears?" Only when we trust to say yes will we find the peace our souls long for.

Passage through the doors that separate us frees us to change, to grow, to love ourselves and others. We must plant our feet in the soil of shared lives to quiet our longing.

All human failures are the result of a lack of love.

— Alfred Adler

How much easier it is to continue working toward a challenging goal when we're bolstered by the loving support of a favorite person, a spouse, or parent. We'll not succeed at every job or game we attempt — nor should we expect to. For all of us our talents are many, but not total. However, our failures will be fewer and far less devastating when they occur within the context of a life rich with loving human contact.

Those who don't know the comfort of love find their steps and thoughts are haunted by the fear that they don't count — that there is no purpose to their lives. Only by knowing the reality of love can we glimpse the richly textured tapestry of human life, and only then can we feel secure that all is well.

One purpose for our lives is to assure others of their importance to the life pattern that captures us all. And when each of us is committed to that purpose, both the fear and the reality of human failure will be erased.

There can be a lot of hurt in love, and there is always risk, and one can't help wondering sometimes if there couldn't be a better way to live.

— Merle Shain

We want to love and be loved, and we mistakenly believe the right significant other will complete our world. The pain and troubling times that fester within a growing, changing relationship aren't really part of the bargain — or so we think — and the decision to stay eludes us sometimes. We run, and then we find ourselves once again longing for completion with another.

What we must understand is that the journey, alone or in partnership, will be uphill at least half the time. But we must also believe the path will only be as rugged as it needs to be to ensure our fullest development.

We simply must trust that it's worth the effort to love, and love some more, even when it hurts, even when we see only darkness at the end of the tunnel. The light will dawn.

Love is something if you give it
away, you end up having more.
                    — Malvina Reynolds

The abundant life appeals to us. Seldom do we want less money, fewer toys, clothes, or friends. In general, we want more of everything and still more — particularly of love. The truth is that the things we hoard or hide or fear losing must be shared or soon may be lost.

Giving love to a lover, a friend, or even a stranger will fill up our own empty spaces where love wants to be. And we'll glow radiantly with the warmth that hovers on the heels of love expressed.

The pantry of the human heart is never bare when love is being served. We pass this way with one another, not by mere chance, but by design for the nourishment that is love.

Our greatest hope, to be loved, is ours when we've made that hope a reality for someone else.

. . . love grows by service.
— Charlotte Perkins Gilman

When we shower someone special with much-needed attention, or maybe flowers, or run an errand for a friend, or volunteer to do a favor for an unnamed person, we benefit in many ways. We're appreciated; we feel good about our own behavior, and we've tightened the connection to another person that fosters personal human development.

Most of us long for more signs of love from one another. Yet we fail to understand that our own expression of love to that special someone will release the love we long to feel.

Love multiplies with frequency of expression, whether stranger to stranger, friend to friend, lover to lover, parent to child; and everyone is the beneficiary.

Love's expression spontaneously generates more of itself, thus promising each of us what we long for.

The more you love, the more love you are given to love with.
— Lucien Price

With love comes promises of sentiment as rapturous as fall's splendor of color and as delicate as a crystal of snow. Love empowers us to handle the struggles that bind us, the struggles that stretch us to grow. The familiar sights and muffled sounds of each moment vibrate with greater intensity when we're giving and receiving love.

We're deluded to think the love of others will complete us, so we strive for it; we long for it. But we receive love only when we're unselfishly offering it. It is one of life's wonderful mysteries that we must first give love away if we hope to get it.

Loving another tests our patience, strength, and security. Love spurned is dreaded and perhaps too familiar, but we must risk it once again if we are to find the love we deserve.

The gifts of love are many — and guaranteed when the act of love is honest, unselfish, whole, and unconditionally offered.

*. . . love is an expanding feeling
that reaches out toward others and
helps them find more abundant life.*
— Lillian Smith

Loneliness visits us all and is seldom perceived as an invitation to share ourselves with others. Yet, what more perfect time to give love to another than when we want to feel love ourselves. Intimacy is one of the gifts of reaching out to someone — friend or stranger.

Knowledge of our wholeness, our oneness with others, and a heightened awareness of how others enrich the fabric of our lives are additional gifts that bless us when we search for connections with others.

The abundance of life is directly proportional to these connections with others. We must choose between closing ourselves off, thus knowing isolation and loneliness, or clasping the hands and hearts of others and knowing the happiness of love.

We all know others who thrive on life. They're alert, eager to talk, to laugh, to love. In their presence we feel necessary.

Love is a positive feeling and if one cultivates this feeling in their life, they will surely free themselves from any unbalanced condition that surrounds them.

— Syd Banks

Anger, whether unfocused or triggered by a troubling experience or a hostile person, discolors our perspective through an afternoon or a full day, perhaps even a week. Our understanding of events is always directly related to the attitude we've chosen to harbor. No situation or person, however difficult, has the power to steal away our happiness without our passive consent.

So willingly we humans adopt negative attitudes. With grandiose egos, we resent rain pouring on our picnic plans or a friend's illness cancelling an engagement. Our choices for actions, feelings, or attitudes are far greater than those we habitually turn to. And it's likely we know love least of all. But just as anger breeds more anger, love cultivates more love, and each life that's touched by love profits from it.

When we make a decision to practice love unconditionally — loving ourselves, our neighbors and co-workers, even the snarling strangers sharing our traffic jam, we'll quickly experience the miracle of love in our own lives.

It is impossible to overemphasize the immense need humans have to be really listened to, to be taken seriously, to be understood.
— Dr. Paul Tournier, M.D.

We need assurance that our presence has value to the lives of those around us at home, work, and play. Our self-worth should not be solely tied to someone else's attention to us or love for us; however, our personal being is validated and thus enhanced each time we have evidence of being fully listened to.

Just as we hunger for attention and validation, so do the many people sharing our travels at this time. And sadly, we're rushing through our experiences not very attentive to either the events or the persons who have engaged our involvement.

The choice to slow down, to honor the flowers, the children, the loud and silent moments of the day, is ours. It's an expression of love for life, for ourselves and everyone we encounter if we take a moment to look and listen with our full being.

Each aspect of life is enriched when honored by a listening heart. Let's cherish the golden rule.

Love immediately challenges me to break the fixation I have with myself.

— John Powell, S.J.

Self-absorption can become habitual, and it's a seductive pastime. "How do I look?" "Was my response articulate?" "Is my wit impressive?" It's all too easy to block out the presence of others except for the purpose of comparison to ourselves. And blocking out their presence robs us of the many lessons they've come to teach us.

The ego is fragile only in proportion to the amount of undue attention we give it. And assuredly we cripple it by the focus we mistakenly believe nurtures its growth. Far better for the health of our ego to love and encourage the well-being of a friend's ego.

The more we move beyond ourselves, the greater will be our personal peace and security. Happiness is the natural byproduct of favoring another with loving attention.

Love cures. It cures those who give it and it cures those who receive it.

— Dr. Karl Menninger

Love is no mystery, but its results are magical in many ways. It's generally accepted that many illnesses are psychosomatic. Because we often feel anxiously alone, lonely, fearful, and unloved, we express our need through our bodies. How sad so many of us are so hindered. But we can each be willing participants in a solution. The action called for is simple. All it requires is the decision to act with favor toward one another.

A look through loving eyes on a struggling person offers her the strength to try and try again and thus succeed. Lovingly moving the barriers to another's achieving spirit will benefit all who share his journey.

Love multiplies the great and simple acts of goodness in the world. Each of us, with no more effort than a genuinely warm glance, can change the course of history today, tomorrow, always.

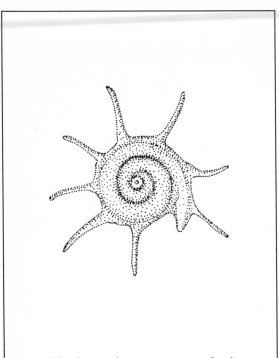

The love, the acceptance of other persons makes me into the unique person I am meant to be.
— Peter G. van Breemen, S.J.

Our destinies are fulfilled through our loving involvement with the men, women, and children sharing our experiences. It is not by accident but by design that we've been drawn together to share goals, the workplace, or a home. We contribute to each other's search for understanding, and the spiritual quest that's at our center finds its resting place in one another's hearts.

The letter, the smile, or phone call we offer a fellow traveler today will bless our own faltering steps throughout the long hours ahead. Each time we focus our attention on the struggle or joy of someone else, our personal well-being is enhanced. If we give away our love, we'll doubt less that we, too, are loved.

Love, and love alone, is capable of giving thee a happier life.
— Ludwig van Beethoven

We are making a response to life every waking moment; our attitudes formulate the tenor of our responses. When the sun warms our bodies and the flowers tease our nostrils, it may be easy to love everyone and smile. When we have a negative attitude, we may snarl and all too quickly criticize innocent bystanders, as well as friends and family. All we need is to make a simple decision to look with love as far as our eyes can see.

When our hearts are God-centered and filled with love and laughter, we'll find no experience too difficult to handle. No problem will evade its solution for long.

An attitude of love promises us gratitude in abundance. We'll never doubt that all is well when love is at our center.

The grand essentials to happiness in this life are something to do, something to love, and something to hope for.

— Joseph Addison

Having someone to bestow our love on — a child, friend, or lover, perhaps a pet — will provide us with a time each day for intimacy, a time for sharing affection, a time which assures us our presence is counted on.

But having someone to love is not all we need for happiness. We must have dreams for the future, reasons for getting out of bed in the present, and the well-earned glow that accompanies past achievements. Dreams lose their glamour if that's all we have. If the reasons for rising don't excite us any longer, or the achievements ring hollow, we'll not come to know the happiness for which we've been created.

Happiness is our birthright so long as we live fully and love truly.

The process rather than the product is primary in caring, for it is only in the present that I can attend to the other.

— Milton Mayeroff

The moment that captures us now is all we have for certain. We can dream endlessly about next week and next year but there are no guarantees. Thus, it is important to care for ourselves and others in this moment. Have we expressed our love to any one of the many special people in our lives today? The effort is small and yet paramount in its impact on how the day unfolds for the givers and the receivers of caring words that inspire — words that speak of love.

Someone close needs our attention today — our encouragement, our inspiration, our recognition. And we need the commitment to focus outside ourselves if we are to discover the gifts promised us in each twenty-four-hour segment of life. It is not coincidence that we feel pulled toward particular people, that we select certain groups to identify with.

Contemplative thoughtfulness about our presence in this time and place will assure us we are needed for the loving growth of many. The mystery unfolds by design.

Our work brings people face to face with love.

— Mother Teresa

Whether we are sowing a garden, tending the sick, role modeling for children, or climbing the corporate ladder, many opportunities are present for acting from a posture of love. Love is an attitude, one born from gratitude for all we have, all we are, and all we hope to be. We cultivate a loving outlook just as surely as we cultivate gardens and friendships.

The guilt or shame we sometimes feel prompts us to remember those moments when we were faced with the choice to love but failed to love — those times we barked answers, scowled at someone special, slammed drawers and doors. Fortunately, we need not be perfect. Each moment promises us a new opportunity to choose love as our response to the many people and the changing events in our lives.

Some decisions can be made once for all time. Using seat belts is such a decision. So is offering love to the world that greets us.